Show Journal

Also available from Sophie Wallace:

- Weekly Planner for Busy People (combining Home and Work)
- Weekly Planner for the Home
- Weekly Meal Planner
- Notebooks
- Sticky Notes Book
- Book of To Do Lists and Big Book of To Do Lists
- A Deerhound Called Rhodry

Copyright © 2017 Sophie Wallace

All rights reserved.

ISBN10: 1544099878

ISBN-13: 978-1544099873

Information

Dog's Name:

Breed: Date of Birth:

Registration Number:

Photo

Sire: Dam:

Breeder:

Microchip Number /   Telephone
Registration Details: Number:

Veterinary Surgeon: Telephone
                                                    Number:

Insurance   Contact
Policy Number: Details:

Awards Won

Award \ Date							
1st							
2nd							
3rd							
Reserve/ 4th							
VHC / 5th							

Awards Won

Award \ Date							
1st							
2nd							
3rd							
Reserve/ 4th							
VHC / 5th							

Awards Won

Award \ Date							
1st							
2nd							
3rd							
Reserve/ 4th							
VHC / 5th							

Awards Won

Award \ Date							
1st							
2nd							
3rd							
Reserve/ 4th							
VHC / 5th							

Awards Won

Award \ Date								
1st								
2nd								
3rd								
Reserve/ 4th								
VHC / 5th								

Awards Won

Date Award							
1st							
2nd							
3rd							
Reserve/ 4th							
VHC / 5th							

Awards Won

Award \ Date								
1st								
2nd								
3rd								
Reserve/ 4th								
VHC / 5th								

Awards Won

Award \ Date							
1st							
2nd							
3rd							
Reserve/ 4th							
VHC / 5th							

Date:	Show:
	Show Society:

Class Entered:	No. of Entrants:
Judge:	No. of Absentees:

Place Details:

1._____

2._____

3._____

4._____

5._____

Other Awards Won:	

Other Classes Entered:	Class:	Judge:
	Placing:	No. Entrants:
		No. of Absentees:

Notes:

Critique Received?		Points Gained:	

Date:	Show:
	Show Society:

Class Entered:	No. of Entrants:
Judge:	No. of Absentees:

Place Details:	1._____
	2._____
	3._____
	4._____
	5._____

Other Awards Won:	

Other Classes Entered:	Class:	Judge:
		No. Entrants:
	Placing:	No. of Absentees:

Notes:

Critique Received?		Points Gained:	

Date:	Show: Show Society:

Class Entered:	No. of Entrants:
Judge:	No. of Absentees:

Place Details:	1._____ 2._____ 3._____ 4._____ 5._____

Other Awards Won:	
Other Classes Entered:	Class: Placing:	Judge: No. Entrants: No. of Absentees:

Notes:

Critique Received?		Points Gained:	

Date:	Show:	
	Show Society:	
Class Entered:		No. of Entrants:
Judge:		No. of Absentees:
Place Details:	1._____ 2._____ 3._____ 4._____ 5._____	
Other Awards Won:		
Other Classes Entered:	Class: Placing:	Judge: No. Entrants: No. of Absentees:
Notes:		
Critique Received?		Points Gained:

Date:	Show:
	Show Society:

Class Entered:	No. of Entrants:
Judge:	No. of Absentees:

Place Details:	1._____
	2._____
	3._____
	4._____
	5._____

Other Awards Won:	

Other Classes Entered:	Class:	Judge:
	Placing:	No. Entrants:
		No. of Absentees:

Notes:

Critique Received?		Points Gained:	

Date:	Show:
	Show Society:

Class Entered:	No. of Entrants:
Judge:	No. of Absentees:

Place Details:	1._____
	2._____
	3._____
	4._____
	5._____

Other Awards Won:	

Other Classes Entered:	Class:	Judge:
	Placing:	No. Entrants:
		No. of Absentees:

Notes:

Critique Received?		Points Gained:	

Date:	Show:
	Show Society:

Class Entered:	No. of Entrants:
Judge:	No. of Absentees:

Place Details:

1._____

2._____

3._____

4._____

5._____

Other Awards Won:

Other Classes Entered:	Class:	Judge:
	Placing:	No. Entrants:
		No. of Absentees:

Notes:

Critique Received?		Points Gained:	

Date:	Show: Show Society:

Class Entered:	No. of Entrants:
Judge:	No. of Absentees:

Place Details:	1._____ 2._____ 3._____ 4._____ 5._____

Other Awards Won:	

Other Classes Entered:	Class: Placing:	Judge: No. Entrants: No. of Absentees:

Notes:

Critique Received?		Points Gained:	

Date:	Show: Show Society:

Class Entered:	No. of Entrants:
Judge:	No. of Absentees:

Place Details:	
	1._____ 2._____ 3._____ 4._____ 5._____

Other Awards Won:	

Other Classes Entered:	Class: Placing:	Judge: No. Entrants: No. of Absentees:

Notes:

Critique Received?		Points Gained:	

Date:	Show:
	Show Society:

Class Entered:	No. of Entrants:
Judge:	No. of Absentees:

Place Details:

1. _____
2. _____
3. _____
4. _____
5. _____

Other Awards Won:	

Other Classes Entered:	Class:	Judge:
	Placing:	No. Entrants:
		No. of Absentees:

Notes:

Critique Received?		Points Gained:	

Date:	Show: Show Society:

Class Entered:	No. of Entrants:
Judge:	No. of Absentees:

Place Details:	
	1._____ 2._____ 3._____ 4._____ 5._____

Other Awards Won:		
Other Classes Entered:	Class: Placing:	Judge: No. Entrants: No. of Absentees:

Notes:

Critique Received?		Points Gained:	

Date:	Show:
	Show Society:

Class Entered:	No. of Entrants:
Judge:	No. of Absentees:

Place Details:	1._____
	2._____
	3._____
	4._____
	5._____

Other Awards Won:	

Other Classes Entered:	Class:	Judge:
	Placing:	No. Entrants:
		No. of Absentees:

Notes:

Critique Received?		Points Gained:	

Date:	Show: Show Society:

Class Entered:	No. of Entrants:
Judge:	No. of Absentees:

Place Details:	1._____ 2._____ 3._____ 4._____ 5._____
Other Awards Won:	

Other Classes Entered:	Class: Placing:	Judge: No. Entrants: No. of Absentees:

Notes:

Critique Received?		Points Gained:	

Date:	Show: Show Society:
Class Entered:	No. of Entrants:
Judge:	No. of Absentees:

Place Details:	1._____ 2._____ 3._____ 4._____ 5._____

Other Awards Won:	
Other Classes Entered:	Class: Placing:	Judge: No. Entrants: No. of Absentees:

Notes:

Critique Received?		Points Gained:	

Date:	Show: Show Society:

Class Entered:	No. of Entrants:
Judge:	No. of Absentees:

Place Details:

1._____

2._____

3._____

4._____

5._____

Other Awards Won:

Other Classes Entered:	Class: Placing:	Judge: No. Entrants: No. of Absentees:

Notes:

Critique Received?		Points Gained:	

Date:	Show: Show Society:
Class Entered:	No. of Entrants:
Judge:	No. of Absentees:
Place Details:	1._____ 2._____ 3._____ 4._____ 5._____
Other Awards Won:	

Other Classes Entered:	Class: Placing:	Judge: No. Entrants: No. of Absentees:

Notes:

Critique Received?		Points Gained:	

Date:	Show: Show Society:
Class Entered:	No. of Entrants:
Judge:	No. of Absentees:

Place Details:	
	1._____ 2._____ 3._____ 4._____ 5._____

Other Awards Won:	

Other Classes Entered:	Class: Placing:	Judge: No. Entrants: No. of Absentees:

Notes:

Critique Received?		Points Gained:	

Date:	Show:
	Show Society:

Class Entered:	No. of Entrants:
Judge:	No. of Absentees:

Place Details:	1._____
	2._____
	3._____
	4._____
	5._____

Other Awards Won:	

Other Classes Entered:	Class:	Judge:
	Placing:	No. Entrants:
		No. of Absentees:

Notes:

Critique Received?		Points Gained:	

Date:	Show:
	Show Society:

Class Entered:	No. of Entrants:
Judge:	No. of Absentees:

Place Details:

1._____

2._____

3._____

4._____

5._____

Other Awards Won:

Other Classes Entered:	Class:	Judge:
	Placing:	No. Entrants:
		No. of Absentees:

Notes:

Critique Received?		Points Gained:	

Date:	Show:	
	Show Society:	
Class Entered:		No. of Entrants:
Judge:		No. of Absentees:
Place Details:	1._____ 2._____ 3._____ 4._____ 5._____	
Other Awards Won:		
Other Classes Entered:	Class: Placing:	Judge: No. Entrants: No. of Absentees:
Notes:		
Critique Received?		Points Gained:

Date:	Show: Show Society:
Class Entered:	No. of Entrants:
Judge:	No. of Absentees:

Place Details:	
	1._____ 2._____ 3._____ 4._____ 5._____

Other Awards Won:	
Other Classes Entered:	Class: Placing:	Judge: No. Entrants: No. of Absentees:

Notes:

Critique Received?		Points Gained:	

Date:	Show:
	Show Society:

Class Entered:	No. of Entrants:
Judge:	No. of Absentees:

Place Details:	1._____
	2._____
	3._____
	4._____
	5._____

Other Awards Won:	

Other Classes Entered:	Class:	Judge:
	Placing:	No. Entrants:
		No. of Absentees:

Notes:			
Critique Received?		Points Gained:	

Date:	Show: Show Society:
Class Entered:	No. of Entrants:
Judge:	No. of Absentees:

Place Details:	1._____ 2._____ 3._____ 4._____ 5._____	
Other Awards Won:		
Other Classes Entered:	Class: Placing:	Judge: No. Entrants: No. of Absentees:
Notes:		
Critique Received?		Points Gained:	

Date:	Show:	
	Show Society:	
Class Entered:		No. of Entrants:
Judge:		No. of Absentees:

Place Details:	1._____
	2._____
	3._____
	4._____
	5._____

Other Awards Won:	

Other Classes Entered:	Class:	Judge:
	Placing:	No. Entrants:
		No. of Absentees:

Notes:

Critique Received?		Points Gained:	

Date:	Show:
	Show Society:

Class Entered:	No. of Entrants:
Judge:	No. of Absentees:

Place Details:	1._____
	2._____
	3._____
	4._____
	5._____

Other Awards Won:	

Other Classes Entered:	Class:	Judge:
	Placing:	No. Entrants:
		No. of Absentees:

Notes:

Critique Received?		Points Gained:	

Date:	Show:
	Show Society:

Class Entered:	No. of Entrants:
Judge:	No. of Absentees:

Place Details:	1._____
	2._____
	3._____
	4._____
	5._____

Other Awards Won:	

Other Classes Entered:	Class:	Judge:
	Placing:	No. Entrants:
		No. of Absentees:

Notes:

Critique Received?		Points Gained:	

Date:	Show: Show Society:
Class Entered:	No. of Entrants:
Judge:	No. of Absentees:

Place Details:	1._____ 2._____ 3._____ 4._____ 5._____
Other Awards Won:	

Other Classes Entered:	Class: Placing:	Judge: No. Entrants: No. of Absentees:

Notes:

Critique Received?		Points Gained:	

Date:	Show:
	Show Society:

Class Entered:	No. of Entrants:
Judge:	No. of Absentees:

Place Details:	1._____
	2._____
	3._____
	4._____
	5._____

Other Awards Won:	

Other Classes Entered:	Class:	Judge:
	Placing:	No. Entrants:
		No. of Absentees:

Notes:

Critique Received?		Points Gained:	

Date:	Show:		
	Show Society:		
Class Entered:		No. of Entrants:	
Judge:		No. of Absentees:	
Place Details:	1._____ 2._____ 3._____ 4._____ 5._____		
Other Awards Won:			
Other Classes Entered:	Class: Placing:	Judge: No. Entrants: No. of Absentees:	
Notes:			
Critique Received?		Points Gained:	

Date:	Show: Show Society:
Class Entered:	No. of Entrants:
Judge:	No. of Absentees:

Place Details:	1._____ 2._____ 3._____ 4._____ 5._____
Other Awards Won:	
Other Classes Entered:	Class: Placing:	Judge: No. Entrants: No. of Absentees:

Notes:

Critique Received?		Points Gained:	

Date:	Show:
	Show Society:

Class Entered:	No. of Entrants:
Judge:	No. of Absentees:

Place Details:	1._____
	2._____
	3._____
	4._____
	5._____

Other Awards Won:	

Other Classes Entered:	Class:	Judge:
		No. Entrants:
	Placing:	No. of Absentees:

Notes:

Critique Received?		Points Gained:	

Date:	Show:
	Show Society:

Class Entered:	No. of Entrants:
Judge:	No. of Absentees:

Place Details:	1._____
	2._____
	3._____
	4._____
	5._____

Other Awards Won:	

Other Classes Entered:	Class:	Judge:
		No. Entrants:
	Placing:	No. of Absentees:

Notes:

Critique Received?		Points Gained:	

Date:	Show: Show Society:
Class Entered:	No. of Entrants:
Judge:	No. of Absentees:

Place Details:	1._____ 2._____ 3._____ 4._____ 5._____
Other Awards Won:	
Other Classes Entered:	Class: Placing:	Judge: No. Entrants: No. of Absentees:

Notes:

| Critique Received? | | Points Gained: | |

Date:	Show:
	Show Society:

Class Entered:	No. of Entrants:
Judge:	No. of Absentees:

Place Details:	1._____
	2._____
	3._____
	4._____
	5._____

Other Awards Won:	

Other Classes Entered:	Class:	Judge:
	Placing:	No. Entrants:
		No. of Absentees:

Notes:

Critique Received?		Points Gained:	

Date:	Show:
	Show Society:

Class Entered:	No. of Entrants:
Judge:	No. of Absentees:

Place Details:	1._____
	2._____
	3._____
	4._____
	5._____

Other Awards Won:	

Other Classes Entered:	Class:	Judge:
		No. Entrants:
	Placing:	No. of Absentees:

Notes:

Critique Received?		Points Gained:	

Date:	Show:	
	Show Society:	
Class Entered:		No. of Entrants:
Judge:		No. of Absentees:
Place Details:	1. _____	
	2. _____	
	3. _____	
	4. _____	
	5. _____	
Other Awards Won:		
Other Classes Entered:	Class:	Judge:
	Placing:	No. Entrants:
		No. of Absentees:
Notes:		
Critique Received?		Points Gained:

Date:	Show:
	Show Society:

Class Entered:	No. of Entrants:
Judge:	No. of Absentees:

Place Details:	1._____
	2._____
	3._____
	4._____
	5._____

Other Awards Won:	

Other Classes Entered:	Class:	Judge:
		No. Entrants:
	Placing:	No. of Absentees:

Notes:

Critique Received?		Points Gained:	

Date:	Show: Show Society:

Class Entered:	No. of Entrants:
Judge:	No. of Absentees:

Place Details:	1._____ 2._____ 3._____ 4._____ 5._____
Other Awards Won:	

Other Classes Entered:	Class: Placing:	Judge: No. Entrants: No. of Absentees:

Notes:

Critique Received?		Points Gained:	

Date:	Show: Show Society:

Class Entered:	No. of Entrants:
Judge:	No. of Absentees:

Place Details:	
	1._____ 2._____ 3._____ 4._____ 5._____

Other Awards Won:	

Other Classes Entered:	Class: Placing:	Judge: No. Entrants: No. of Absentees:

Notes:

Critique Received?		Points Gained:	

Date:	Show:
	Show Society:

Class Entered:	No. of Entrants:
Judge:	No. of Absentees:

Place Details:	1._____
	2._____
	3._____
	4._____
	5._____

Other Awards Won:	

Other Classes Entered:	Class:	Judge:
		No. Entrants:
	Placing:	No. of Absentees:

Notes:

Critique Received?		Points Gained:	

Date:	Show:	
	Show Society:	
Class Entered:		No. of Entrants:
Judge:		No. of Absentees:

Place Details:	1._____
	2._____
	3._____
	4._____
	5._____

Other Awards Won:	

Other Classes Entered:	Class:	Judge:
		No. Entrants:
	Placing:	No. of Absentees:

Notes:

Critique Received?		Points Gained:	

Date:	Show:
	Show Society:

Class Entered:	No. of Entrants:
Judge:	No. of Absentees:

Place Details:	1._____
	2._____
	3._____
	4._____
	5._____

Other Awards Won:	

Other Classes Entered:	Class:	Judge:
	Placing:	No. Entrants:
		No. of Absentees:

Notes:

Critique Received?		Points Gained:	

Date:	Show: Show Society:
Class Entered:	No. of Entrants:
Judge:	No. of Absentees:

Place Details:	1._____ 2._____ 3._____ 4._____ 5._____
Other Awards Won:	

Other Classes Entered:	Class: Placing:	Judge: No. Entrants: No. of Absentees:

Notes:

Critique Received?		Points Gained:	

Date:	Show: Show Society:

Class Entered:	No. of Entrants:
Judge:	No. of Absentees:

Place Details:	1._____ 2._____ 3._____ 4._____ 5._____

Other Awards Won:		
Other Classes Entered:	Class: Placing:	Judge: No. Entrants: No. of Absentees:

Notes:

Critique Received?		Points Gained:	

Date:	Show: Show Society:
Class Entered:	No. of Entrants:
Judge:	No. of Absentees:

Place Details:	1._____ 2._____ 3._____ 4._____ 5._____

Other Awards Won:	

Other Classes Entered:	Class: Placing:	Judge: No. Entrants: No. of Absentees:

Notes:

Critique Received?		Points Gained:	

Date:	Show: Show Society:
Class Entered:	No. of Entrants:
Judge:	No. of Absentees:

Place Details:	1._____ 2._____ 3._____ 4._____ 5._____

Other Awards Won:	
Other Classes Entered:	Class: Placing:	Judge: No. Entrants: No. of Absentees:

Notes:

Critique Received?		Points Gained:	

Date:	Show:
	Show Society:

Class Entered:	No. of Entrants:
Judge:	No. of Absentees:

Place Details:	1._____
	2._____
	3._____
	4._____
	5._____

Other Awards Won:	

Other Classes Entered:	Class:	Judge:
		No. Entrants:
	Placing:	No. of Absentees:

Notes:

Critique Received?		Points Gained:	

| Date: | Show: |
| | Show Society: |

| Class Entered: | No. of Entrants: |
| Judge: | No. of Absentees: |

Place Details:	1._____
	2._____
	3._____
	4._____
	5._____

| Other Awards Won: | |

Other Classes Entered:	Class:	Judge:
	Placing:	No. Entrants:
		No. of Absentees:

Notes:

| Critique Received? | | Points Gained: | |

Date:	Show: Show Society:
Class Entered:	No. of Entrants:
Judge:	No. of Absentees:

Place Details:	
	1._____ 2._____ 3._____ 4._____ 5._____

Other Awards Won:	

Other Classes Entered:	Class: Placing:	Judge: No. Entrants: No. of Absentees:

Notes:

Critique Received?		Points Gained:	

Date:	Show:
	Show Society:

Class Entered:	No. of Entrants:
Judge:	No. of Absentees:

Place Details:	1._____
	2._____
	3._____
	4._____
	5._____

Other Awards Won:	

Other Classes Entered:	Class:	Judge:
	Placing:	No. Entrants:
		No. of Absentees:

Notes:

Critique Received?		Points Gained:	

Date:	Show: Show Society:

Class Entered:	No. of Entrants:
Judge:	No. of Absentees:

Place Details:	1._____ 2._____ 3._____ 4._____ 5._____

Other Awards Won:	
Other Classes Entered:	Class: Placing:	Judge: No. Entrants: No. of Absentees:

Notes:

Critique Received?		Points Gained:	

Date:	Show:
	Show Society:

Class Entered:	No. of Entrants:
Judge:	No. of Absentees:

Place Details:

1._____
2._____
3._____
4._____
5._____

Other Awards Won:	

Other Classes Entered:	Class:	Judge:
	Placing:	No. Entrants:
		No. of Absentees:

Notes:

Critique Published?		Points Gained:	

Date:	Show: Show Society:
Class Entered:	No. of Entrants:
Judge:	No. of Absentees:

Place Details:	1._____ 2._____ 3._____ 4._____ 5._____

Other Awards Won:		
Other Classes Entered:	Class: Placing:	Judge: No. Entrants: No. of Absentees:

Notes:

Critique Received?		Points Gained:	

| Date: | Show: |
| | Show Society: |

Class Entered:	No. of Entrants:
Judge:	No. of Absentees:

Place Details:

1._____

2._____

3._____

4._____

5._____

Other Awards Won:

Other Classes Entered:	Class:	Judge:
	Placing:	No. Entrants:
		No. of Absentees:

Notes:

| Critique Published? | | Points Gained: | |

Critiques

Show:

Date:

Judge:

Critique:

Show:

Date:

Judge:

Critique:

Show:

Date:

Judge:

Critique:

Show:	Judge:
Date:	

Critique:

Show:	Judge:
Date:	

Critique:

Show:	Judge:
Date:	

Critique:

Show:	Judge:
Date:	

Critique:

Show:	Judge:
Date:	

Critique:

Show:	Judge:
Date:	

Critique:

Show:	Judge:
Date:	

Critique:

Show:	Judge:
Date:	

Critique:

Show:	Judge:
Date:	

Critique:

Show:	Judge:
Date:	

Critique:

Show:	Judge:
Date:	

Critique:

Show:	Judge:
Date:	

Critique:

Show:	Judge:
Date:	

Critique:

Show:	Judge:
Date:	

Critique:

Show:	Judge:
Date:	

Critique:

Show:	Judge:
Date:	

Critique:

Show:	Judge:
Date:	

Critique:

Show:	Judge:
Date:	

Critique:

Show:	Judge:
Date:	

Critique:

Show:	Judge:
Date:	

Critique:

Show:	Judge:
Date:	

Critique:

Show:	Judge:
Date:	

Critique:

Show:	Judge:
Date:	

Critique:

Show:	Judge:
Date:	

Critique:

Show:	Judge:
Date:	

Critique:

Show:	Judge:
Date:	

Critique:

Show:	Judge:
Date:	

Critique:

Show:	Judge:
Date:	

Critique:

Show:	Judge:
Date:	

Critique:

Show:	Judge:
Date:	

Critique:

Show:	Judge:
Date:	

Critique:

Show:	Judge:
Date:	

Critique:

Show:	Judge:
Date:	

Critique:

Show:	Judge:
Date:	

Critique:

Show:	Judge:
Date:	

Critique:

Show:	Judge:
Date:	

Critique:

Show:	Judge:
Date:	

Critique:

Show:	Judge:
Date:	

Critique:

Show:	Judge:
Date:	

Critique:

Show:	Judge:
Date:	

Critique:

Show:	Judge:
Date:	

Critique:

Show:	Judge:
Date:	

Critique:

Show:	Judge:
Date:	

Critique:

Show:	Judge:
Date:	

Critique:

Show:	Judge:
Date:	

Critique:

Judge Information	Judge	Show Under Again?		Details
		Yes	No	
Date:				
Show:				
Date:				
Show:				
Date:				
Show:				
Date:				
Show:				
Date:				
Show:				

Judge Information	Judge	Show Under Again?		Details
		Yes	No	
Date:				
Show:				
Date:				
Show:				
Date:				
Show:				
Date:				
Show:				
Date:				
Show:				

Judge Information	Judge	Show Under Again?		Details
		Yes	No	
Date: Show:				
Date: Show:				
Date: Show:				
Date: Show:				
Date: Show:				

Judge Information	Judge	Show Under Again?		Details
		Yes	No	
Date:				
Show:				
Date:				
Show:				
Date:				
Show:				
Date:				
Show:				
Date:				
Show:				

Judge Information	Judge	Show Under Again?		Details
		Yes	No	
Date:				
Show:				
Date:				
Show:				
Date:				
Show:				
Date:				
Show:				
Date:				
Show:				

Judge Information	Judge	Show Under Again?		Details
		Yes	No	
Date: Show:				
Date: Show:				
Date: Show:				
Date: Show:				
Date: Show:				

Judge Information	Judge	Show Under Again?		Details
		Yes	No	
Date:				
Show:				
Date:				
Show:				
Date:				
Show:				
Date:				
Show:				
Date:				
Show:				

Judge Information	Judge	Show Under Again?		Details
		Yes	No	
Date:				
Show:				
Date:				
Show:				
Date:				
Show:				
Date:				
Show:				
Date:				
Show:				

Judge Information	Judge	Show Under Again?		Details
		Yes	No	
Date:				
Show:				
Date:				
Show:				
Date:				
Show:				
Date:				
Show:				
Date:				
Show:				

Judge Information	Judge	Show Under Again?		Details
		Yes	No	
Date:				
Show:				
Date:				
Show:				
Date:				
Show:				
Date:				
Show:				
Date:				
Show:				

Judge Information	Judge	Show Under Again?		Details
		Yes	No	
Date:				
Show:				
Date:				
Show:				
Date:				
Show:				
Date:				
Show:				
Date:				
Show:				

Judge Information	Judge	Show Under Again?		Details
		Yes	No	
Date:				
Show:				
Date:				
Show:				
Date:				
Show:				
Date:				
Show:				
Date:				
Show:				

Glossary of Showing Terms – United Kingdom

Class Types

MP	Minor Puppy- For dogs of six and not exceeding nine calendar months of age on the first day of the show
P	Puppy- For dogs of six and not exceeding twelve calendar months of age on the first day of the show
J	Junior- For dogs of six and not exceeding eighteen calendar months on the first day of the show
Y	Yearling- For dogs of twelve and not exceeding twenty four calendar months on the first day of the show
B	Beginner- For owner, handler or exhibit not having won a first prize at a Championship or Open Show
M	Maiden- For dogs which have not won a Challenge Certificate or a First Prize at an Open or Championship Show (excluding MP, Special MP, Puppy and Special Puppy classes- whether restricted or not)
N	Novice- For dogs which have not won a Challenge Certificate or three or more First prizes at Open or Championship Shows (excluding MP, Special MP, Puppy and Special Puppy classes- whether restricted or not)
UG	Under Graduate- For dogs which have not won a Challenge Certificate or three or more First Prizes at Championship Shows where Challenge Certificates were offered for the breed (excluding MP, Special MP, Puppy and Special Puppy classes- whether restricted or not)
G	Graduate- For dogs which have not won a Challenge Certificate or four or more First Prizes at Championship Shows in Graduate, Post Graduate, Minor Limit, Mid Limit, Limit and Open Classes, whether restricted or not where Challenge Certificates were offered for the breed

PG	Post Graduate – For dogs which have not won a Challenge Certificate or five or more First Prizes at Championship Shows in Post Graduate, Minor Limit, Mid Limit, Limit and Open Classes, whether restricted or not where Challenge Certificates were offered for the breed
L	Limit – For dogs which have not become show Champions under the Kennel Club Regulations or under the rules of any Governing Body recognised by the Kennel Club, or won 7 or more First Prizes in all at Championship Shows in Limit or Open Classes confined to the Breed, whether restricted or not at Shows where Challenge Certificates were offered for the breed.
O	Open – For all dogs of the breeds for which the class is provided and eligible for entry at the show
V	Veteran – For dogs of not less than seven years of age on the first day of the show
AV	Any Variety
AVNSC	Any Variety Not Separately Classified
IR	Import Register
JH	Junior Handler
NFC	Not For Competition

Award Types

BP	Best Puppy	BD	Best Dog
BB	Best Bitch	BOS	Best Opposite Sex
BPIB	Best Puppy in Breed	RBOB	Reserve Best of Breed
BOB	Best of Breed	BIG	Best in Group
RBIS	Reserve Best in Show	BIS	Best in Show
CC	Challenge Certificate	RCC	Reserve Challenge Certificate

Showing Information- United States

Class Types
Puppy 6-9 Months
Puppy 9-12 Months
Twelve to Fifteen Months
Fifteen to Eighteen Months
Novice
Amateur Owner Handler
Bred by Exhibitor
American Bred
Open

Award Types
Reserve Winners Dog   Reserve Winners Bitch
Winners Dog   Winners Bitch
Best of Breed
Best Opposite Sex
Best of Winners
Best in Group
Reserve Best in Show
Best in Show

Notes

Notes

Notes

ABOUT THE AUTHOR

Sophie Wallace currently lives in rural Yorkshire with her family and a selection of animals. She combines working with writing books including the bestselling children's book "A Deerhound called Rhodry" and a range of Planners and Journals.

Sophie enjoys showing the family Deerhound, Druss and they have been to Crufts three times. A new puppy has just joined the family, and Sophie decided to design this Show Journal to record his progress at shows. Having all the information in one place will make it easy to see which classes he is eligible to enter.

Be the first to know about new additions to Sophie's range of planners and books by following her on:

Twitter: @YorkshireClerk
Facebook: Sophie Wallace Author @SophieWallaceAuthor
Sophie's Amazon Author page

As well as this Show Journal, Sophie's range includes Home and Work Planners (to juggle home and work life), the Home Planner and notebooks in a variety of beautiful covers.

Sophie would love to hear from you so please do get in touch if you would like to chat about the planners or make any suggestions for future editions.

Printed in Great Britain
by Amazon